IMAGES
Nature

Concept and text:
Émilie Beaumont

Marie-Renée Pimont
primary school teacher

Illustrations:
Vivienne Bray, N. Le Guillouzic,
F. Guiraud

Translation:
Lara M. Andahazy

FLEURUS

TABLE OF CONTENTS

ANIMALS 7

TREES 39

FLOWERS AND PLANTS 69

WEATHER 93

WATER 109

ROCKS AND LANDFORMS 119

ANIMALS

COLTS GROW QUICKLY!

Something wonderful has happened in the stable—a baby horse was just born. Look! The colt can already stand up.

A stallion and a mare have to meet in order to produce a foal.

Baby horses grow in their mothers' tummies for ten months.

When the mare gives birth, a colt or filly comes out front feet first.

Mother licks her baby clean. After a few minutes the foal can stand up. It will soon nurse.

THE BIRTH OF A CHICK

Mother chicken lays an egg—but don't eat it! A surprise is growing.

Father rooster meets mother hen in the farmyard.

Mother hen lays an egg in her nest of straw.

Mother hen sits on her egg to keep it warm.

The baby chick breaks out of its egg!

INSIDE THE EGG

Little by little the chick grows to fill the egg shell.
The egg yolk that nourishes the chick disappears!

You can see the chick embryo after just one week.

The chick is well-formed after two weeks.

All is ready after only three weeks!

And here is a baby chick ready to nibble up grain.

HOW BABY KANGAROOS ARE BORN

Baby kangaroos are tiny at birth. Luckily their mothers carry them warm and snug in their pouches for a long time.

Papa and mama kangaroo have just mated.

One month later, mama kangaroo leans against a tree with her tail pulled up in front.

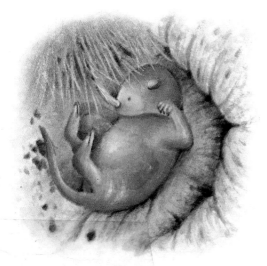

She pushes her baby out into her pouch where it can nurse.

She will carry her baby in her pouch for six months.

FROM TADPOLE TO FROG

What a lot goes on in the pond! It all starts
when a mother frog and a father frog meet.

The female lays
thousand of eggs.

Small tadpoles come
out of the eggs.

They swim by
wagging their tails.

Two long webbed
feet appear.

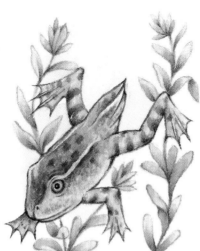

Their tails get shorter
and they grow front
legs.

The tadpole has turned
into a frog and can leave
the water.

13

FROM CATERPILLAR TO BUTTERFLY

When you come across a caterpillar can you imagine it turning into a butterfly?

A male and a female butterfly mate.

The female lays her eggs on a leaf.

Out comes a hungry caterpillar.

It wraps itself in a cocoon and turns into...

a beautiful butterfly with folded wings.

The butterfly cleans its wings and flies away.

HOW ARE SNAILS BORN?

There are no papa and mama snails. Every snail is both male and female at the same time and can lay eggs.

The snail sets out in search of a mate.

The two snails bodies join together.

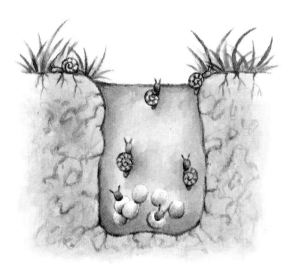

The snail's eggs come out of a hole behind its horns.

Baby snails' shells are transparent at birth.

THEIR BABIES COME FROM EGGS

In the animal kingdom many females lay eggs—small or large eggs, soft or hard eggs.

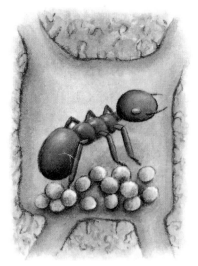

Father penguins sit on the eggs.

Queen ants lay eggs every day.

Fish lay thousands of eggs.

il coccodrillo
Baby crocodiles use a special tooth to break out of their eggs.

Snakes' egg shells are soft but very strong.

TO EACH HIS OWN HOME
Many animals make nests for their children.

Swallows make their nests out of mud and straw.

Field mice make their nests out of grass.

Wasps chew up tiny pieces of wood to make the walls of their hives.

Chaffinches use twigs and moss.

Sticklebacks are the only fish that make nests. They use bits of plants.

WHAT ODD ANIMALS!

You have probably never run into one of these odd animals. They live in the oceans or in distant countries.

Iguanas are giant lizards that live in the Galapagos Islands.

Armadillos have thick armor and strong claws.

Anteaters catch termites and ants with their long, sticky tongues.

Duck-billed platypuses are good swimmers. They lay eggs.

What a funny place for the hammer-head shark's eyes!

Octopuses spread clouds of ink in the water when they are scared.

Uakari monkeys are almost bald and have red faces.

Molochs are also called "mountain demons."

SPIDER WEBS

A sort of liquid that hardens in the air comes out of spiders' stomachs. This is the thread they use to weave webs.

First the spider makes a silk frame.

Then it weaves the spokes according to a precise plan.

It then builds a spiral with the sticky thread by starting in the center.

The spider eats the flies that get trapped in its web.

GET TO WORK, ANTS!

Ants work tirelessly to gather food.
They sleep through the winter in their anthills.

Ants can carry objects bigger
than they are.

When their prey is too heavy
they help each other.

Ants raise aphids to "milk"
them of their honey.

Food is carefully stocked
in the anthill.

BEAVERS—CLEAVER BUILDERS

Beavers build dams to hold back water. This way they can build their homes out of the way of currents.

Beavers nibble away tree trunks with their strong front teeth.

Their dams are made out of logs held together by mud.

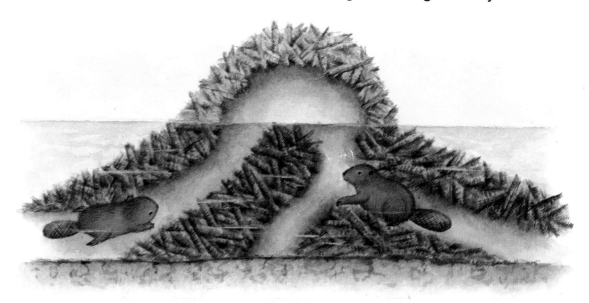

Beavers enter their homes through hidden underwater tunnels. Their bedrooms are snug and dry. They line them with grass and wood chips.

BUSY BEES

All the bees in the hive work hard. They change jobs as they get older.

Gatherers collect a sweet liquid—flower nectar.

Workers secrete wax to make the alveoli.

The queen lays an egg in each alveolus.

Nurse bees take good care of the larvae that grow into bees.

SHH! THEY'RE SLEEPING

Depending on where they live, animals have different tricks to get a good night's sleep.

Koalas sleep well clinging to their trees.

Macaque monkeys snuggle together.

Parrot fish secrete a sticky substance that protects them.

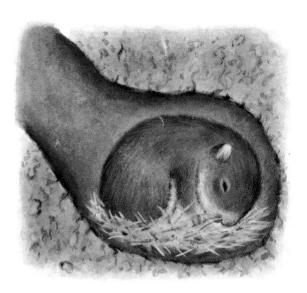

Hamsters sleep safe and snug in their burrows.

Mother gorillas sleep sitting up
with their babies in their arms.

Giraffes can sleep standing up.

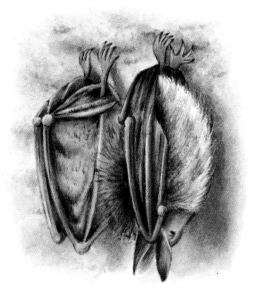

Bats hang upside
down to sleep.

Lions sleep hidden in
tall grass.

THEY LIVE A LONG TIME

If they don't get sick or caught by their enemies,
these animals live a long time.

Cockatoos can live seventy years
and giant turtles more than one
hundred.

Elephants can live around
sixty years.

Sturgeons can live more
than 100 years.

Chimpanzees live for fifty
years.

SHORT LIVES!

These animals' lives are very short. But it takes some of them—like the mayfly—several months to become adults.

Shrews are the size of a mouse and live for about one year.

Seahorses—those strange fish—live for about one year.

Adult mayflies live only for one or two days.

Butterflies live for less than a year and fly less than a month.

THEIR FAVORITE FOODS

Every animal has its own way of catching and eating its favorite foods—fruits, insects or small animals.

Mother birds catch insects for their babies.

Some snakes strangle their prey in their coils before eating it.

Squirrels nibble walnuts, hazelnuts and acorns with their sharp front teeth.

Raccoons "wash" their food before eating it. They like frogs and fish.

Giraffes eat the tender leaves on the tops of trees.

Chimpanzees like to eat fruit, leaves and termites.

Lions hunt zebras, African buffaloes and antelopes.

Rhinoceroses graze on the savannah grasses.

RECORD BREAKERS

Have an adult help you compare these speeds and distances with ones you know—the speed of a car or the height of a tree.

Peregrine falcons swoop down on their prey at 175 m.p.h.

Ostriches can easily run 30 m.p.h.

Large kangaroos can jump more than 30 feet.

Hares can jump more than 20 feet.

Pumas can jump up onto a
branch 15 feet high.

Dolphins can jump 16 feet up
out of the water.

Gibbon monkeys can jump onto
branches 25 feet away.

It takes only two seconds for
running cheetahs to reach 45 m.p.h.

UNDERGROUND TUNNELS

There is a whole world living under the ground.
Every once in a while a tiny nose pokes out for a breath of fresh air.

Moles are nearly blind and live underground.
They dig tunnels with small piles of dirt called molehills at the entrances.

Shrews dig underground tunnels and eat the roots of plants.
They also store food for winter.

UNDERGROUND ANIMALS

Lots of different animals dig underground tunnels that let in the air they breathe.

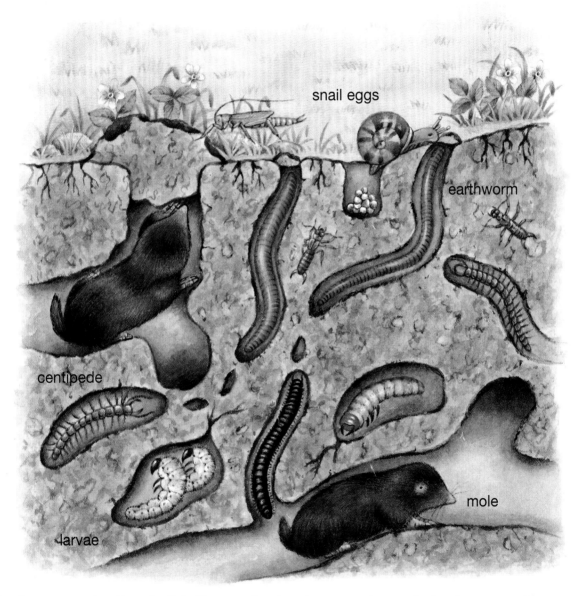

snail eggs

earthworm

centipede

mole

larvae

Earthworms don't eat dirt, they eat microbes, roots and plants.
Centipedes love to eat snails.

ANIMALS FROM COLD COUNTRIES

All these animals live near the poles.
Their fur coats and thick layers of fat keep them warm in winter.

Penguins are birds that can't fly—but they can swim.

Wolves have thick fur. They hunt at night.

This huge walrus has two long ivory tusks.

Seals' thick skins protect them as they slide on the ice.

Polar bears' long white fur
coats keep them warm.

Reindeer dig under the snow to
find grass to eat during the winter.

Polar foxes' fur coats are white in
winter and gray in summer.

Lemmings—no bigger than rats—
live near the North Pole.

ANIMALS FROM HOT COUNTRIES

These animals live in the savannah or the jungle and know where to find water.

Lions are very strong and handsome— they are the "kings of the jungle."

Crocodiles are very heavy but can move very fast.

Hippopotamuses spend their days in ponds in order to keep cool.

Rhinoceroses are grouchy animals but they can't see very well.

Elephants take showers to wash off bothersome insects.

Giraffes are the tallest animals in the world.

Gazelles can run very quickly to escape their enemies.

Chimpanzees drink the water that gathers in hollow tree trunks.

ARMS, HEADS AND TAILS THAT GROW BACK

These animals don't worry when they lose a body part. It will grow back.

When starfish lose an arm it grows back quickly.

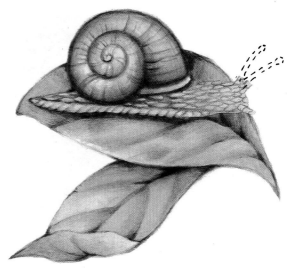

When snails lose their heads they can grow new ones.

Lizards can grow new tails if they lose theirs.

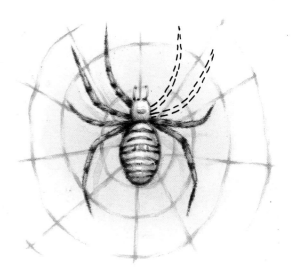

When spiders lose a leg or two they can grow new ones.

TREES

A TREE—FROM TOP TO BOTTOM
Can you point to the different parts of a tree: the treetop, the roots, the trunk, a branch, the leaves and the bark?

1 - treetop
2 - trunk
3 - bark

4 - branch
5 - leaves
6 - roots

THE BIRTH OF AN OAK TREE

Oak trees start with a tiny acorn. Below are all the different stages of their birth.

It all starts with a partially buried acorn. Inside it are two cotyledons full of food.

When spring comes a root pierces the acorn shell and grows down into the ground.

A stem grows up out of the ground and tiny leaves appear.

Young oak trees need sunlight and water to grow.

TREES ARE ALIVE

You need to eat and drink in order to grow big and strong—so do trees!
Their sap feeds them.

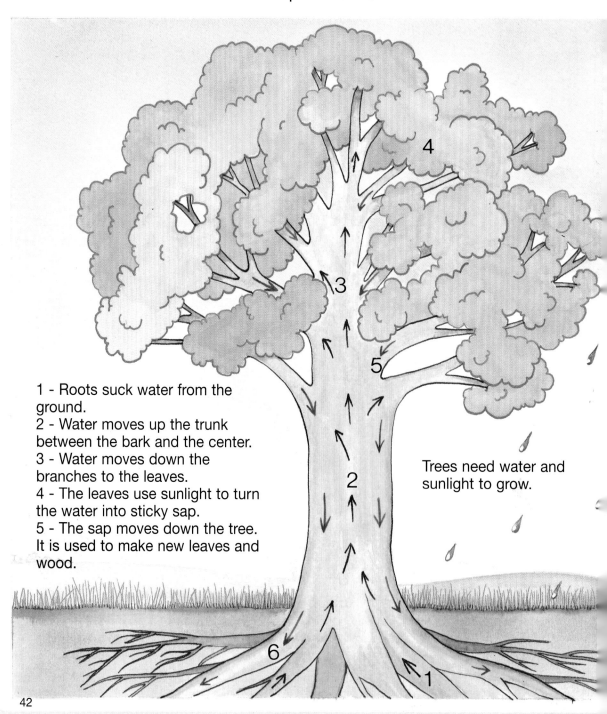

1 - Roots suck water from the ground.
2 - Water moves up the trunk between the bark and the center.
3 - Water moves down the branches to the leaves.
4 - The leaves use sunlight to turn the water into sticky sap.
5 - The sap moves down the tree. It is used to make new leaves and wood.

Trees need water and sunlight to grow.

No, this tiny tree won't break! Its trunk will get thicker and become strong and hard. Bark will grow over it and protect it.

Wood that grows in spring forms light rings and wood that grows in summer makes dark rings. You can tell how old a tree is by counting the dark rings.

- The extra sap is ored in the roots to lp next year's aves grow.

A SPRING SURPRISE!

Tiny buds don't seem to grow during the winter but they are preparing a wonderful spring surprise for us!

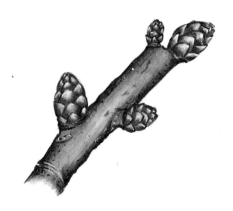

Buds have scales that act like armor against rain and ice.

You can see the tiny leaves folded inside the bud. Fuzz protects them from the cold.

When spring comes, sap moves up the tree to the buds. Their scales open little by little.

The tiny leaves unfold. The leaves will grow and the buds will disappear.

A SPIDER LEAF

You can make a spider leaf by pulling off the flat part, the lamina. All that's left are the veins or nervures!

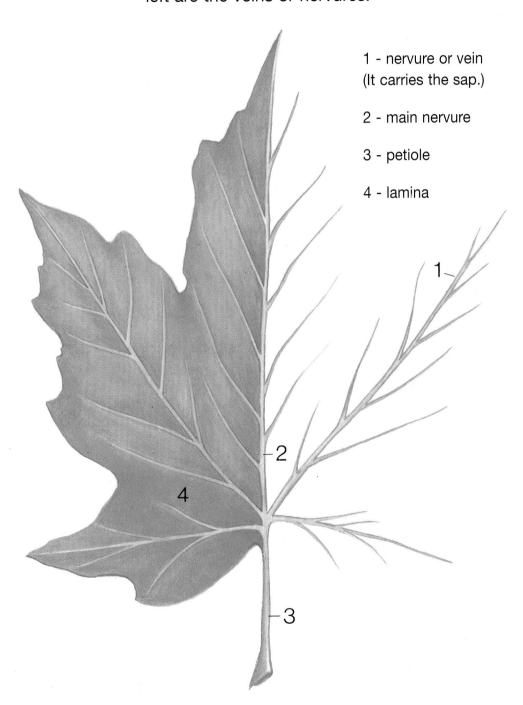

1 - nervure or vein
(It carries the sap.)

2 - main nervure

3 - petiole

4 - lamina

FOUR SEASONS FOR A CHESTNUT TREE

Look at all the changes that take place in this chestnut tree
and all around it from one spring to the next.

Leaves and flowers come out of the buds in spring.

Chestnuts grow in their husks during the summer.

Leaves and chestnuts fall to the ground in autumn.

The chestnut tree rests in winter. It is waiting for spring.

THEY STAY GREEN ALL YEAR

These trees also lose their needles but never all at once. Needles fall and new ones grow all year long.

pine tree

spruce tree

cedar tree

cypress tree

47

DECIDUOUS OR EVERGREEN

The leaves of deciduous trees fall in autumn but not the leaves (or needles) of evergreen trees. Do you know why?

A lot of water evaporates out of the leaves of this tree. If the tree kept its leaves it would use up all its reserves.

Pine needles are tiny and lose very little water so the tree can keep them all winter long.

IN THE SHADE OR IN THE SUN

All living creatures need sunlight. What happens when part
of a tree doesn't get any sun?

The middle tree has kept
only its highest branches.
The others didn't get any
sunlight so they fell off. ▶

◀ The trees at the edge of
the forest grow bigger
branches on the sunny
side.

▼ This tree gets lots of
sunlight—branches grow
all around it.

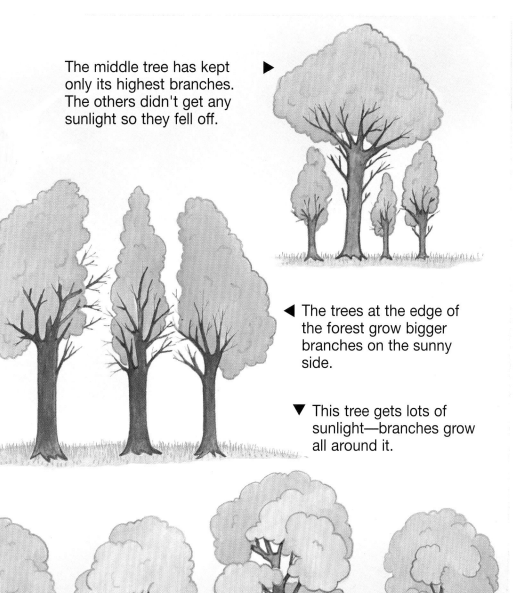

LEARN TO RECOGNIZE DIFFERENT TREES

You can recognize different kinds of trees by their fruits or nuts and by their leaves. These pictures can help you.

This is an OAK tree: part of its nut, the acorn, is covered with a cap, the cupule.

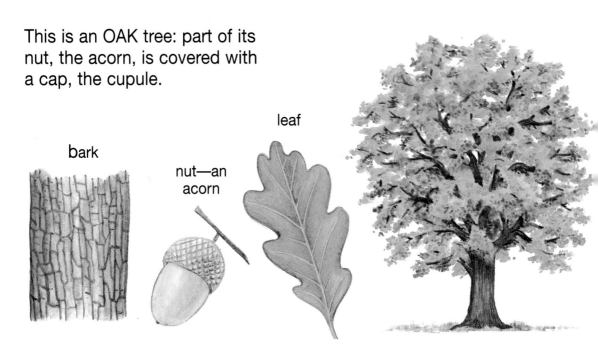

bark

nut—an acorn

leaf

This is a CHESTNUT tree. Its nuts—chestnuts—are covered by a thin husk.

bark

chestnut

leaf

This is a BEECH tree.
Several forest animals eat
beech nuts.

bark

beechnut

leaf

This is a PINE tree.
It stays green all year long.
That's why pine trees are
used as Christmas trees.

pine cone

pine needles

bark

This is a BIRCH tree. Tiny seeds grow
in its female cones, called catkins.
Male catkins are long and thin.

lacy leaf

Silver bark

male catkins

This is a LINDEN tree.
People dry its flowers
and leaves to make tea.

bark

linden
seeds—the
size of
a pea

heart-shaped leaf

a poplar tree

an ash tree

a hornbeam tree

a weeping willow

a plane tree

THE TALLEST TREES

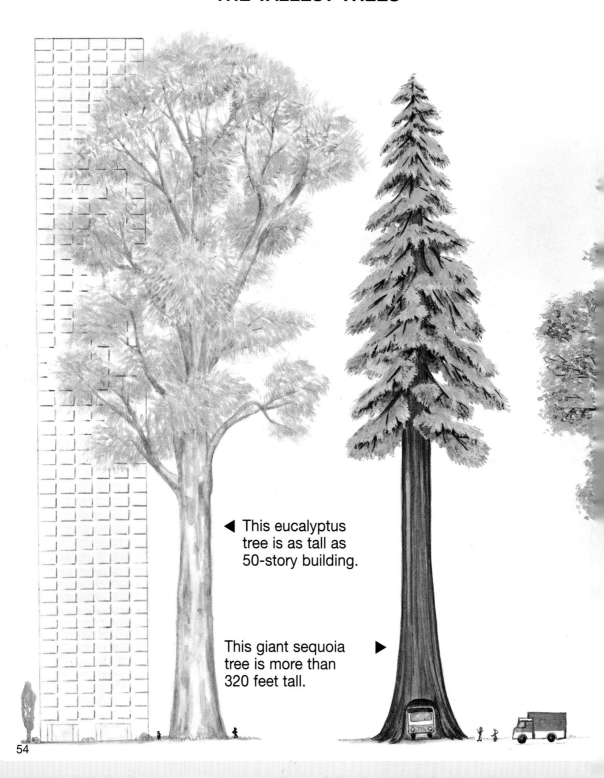

◄ This eucalyptus tree is as tall as 50-story building.

This giant sequoia tree is more than 320 feet tall. ►

54

THE BIGGEST TREE
It would take twenty people holding hands to make a ring around this baobab tree.

Bonsais are real trees that people trim to keep them small.

ginkgo leaf

The first ginkgo trees appeared during the dinosaur age.

55

FRUIT TREES

These trees love sunshine. They can be found in warm countries.
How many can you name?

fig tree

date tree

olive tree

lemon tree

banana tree

coconut tree

These trees are very common in our country. Can you name them all?
Do you like their fruit?

cherry tree

apple tree

pear tree

plum tree

peach tree

hazelnut tree 57

ENDANGERED FORESTS

Forests all around the world are threatened by pollution, fire and deforestation.

People are rapidly cutting down the Amazon forests...

to make fields.

In the Sahara, men need lumber but...

they cut down too many trees and the desert is growing.

Factory chimneys spew out chemical products...

that fall on forests as acid rain.

Forest fires spread quickly during the dry season.

It takes many years for the trees to grow back.

WOODWORK

Lumberjacks know forest trees very well.
They choose trees that will be useful for carpenters.

Lumberjacks cut down
the trees marked with white.

Trucks carry the tree trunks
to the sawmill.

At the sawmill, large saws cut
the tree trunks into planks of wood.

Carpenters turn
the planks into
pretty furniture.

TREES GIVE US ALL THIS!

Here are just a few of the things we can make out of tree trunks or bark.
How many more things can you name?

Paper is made out of wood fibers.

Games and toys are made out of painted wood.

Many things can be made out of the bark of cork-oak trees.

It took many planks of wood to make this boat.

WHAT DO TREES DO?

Trees make the oxygen that people and animals need.
They do many other things too.

Water evaporates from tree leaves and forms new clouds in the sky.

Many animals live in the shelter of forests.

Trees protect houses from ocean winds.

Trees can slow down and stop avalanches.

TREES AND THE SEASONS

Tell this tree's story. What happens to it during each season?
Match each large picture to a small one and explain why.

PROTECT THE FORESTS

You can become a forest friend by following a few simple rules.
Teach your family and friends the rules too.

Gather up all your trash after each picnic.
Don't leave any trash in the forest.

Be careful not to crush saplings. They might grow into beautiful trees.

This Christmas tree was grown in a tree nursery, not in the forest. Don't cut down pine trees in the forest.

Bark protects the trees' trunks. Don't hurt it!

Forest fires spread quickly. Don't light fires in the woods!

Don't leave broken glass on the ground. It could cause a forest fire!

Forest fires can start with just one lit cigarette thrown out of a car window.

AUTUMN LEAVES
It is easy to dry leaves to make bouquets or decorate pictures.
Here's how:

You need a large catalog
with lots of pages.

Carefully slip each leaf
between two pages.

Make sure you chose
clean, whole leaves.

Close the catalog and put a
heavy weight on top of it.

After a week your leaves will be dry
and you can use them to decorate your room.

MIX AND MATCH
Name each picture. Next, match each nut with the right leaf.

MAKE A BOUQUET OUT OF DRY LEAVES

Leaves turn pretty colors in autumn. Gather a few and make them into a bouquet that will last all winter long.

Cut leaves with their stems.

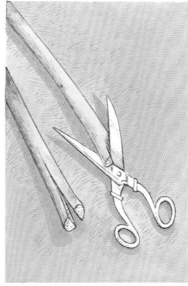

Cut a slit in the stems with a pair of scissors.

Use one cup of glycerine for every two cups of water.

Pour the water and glycerine into a jar.

Let the leaves soak for ten days.

Last, put your leaves in a pretty vase.

FLOWERS
AND PLANTS

SCIENTIFIC FLOWER WORDS

Corolla and calyx—these special words and others are the names of flower parts. Discover them below.

Parts of a flower:

1. The corolla is made up of the flower's petals.

2. The sepals make up the calyx.

3. the stem

4. a leaf

5. the roots

A closer look at the heart of a flower:

1. The petals protect the stamens.

2. The stamens carry the pollen.

3. The sepals protect the pistil.

4. the pistil

Pollen lands on the pistil. Seeds form after fertilization. They will grow into new flowers.

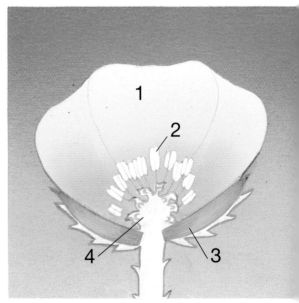

THE BIRTH OF A HYACINTH

Buy a hyacinth bulb in the beginning of winter and follow the advice below.
You will have a beautiful flower in winter.

Fill a glass jar to the top with water.

Put the bulb flat-side down over the opening of the jar.

Cover the jar with a large box.

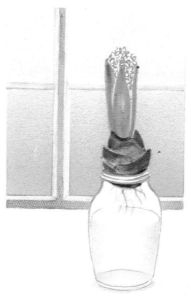

Three weeks later you will see small roots.

Then put the jar near a window.

Your hyacinth will flower about three weeks later.

A DANDELION'S STORY

Each large dandelion is made up of hundreds of tiny flowers squeezed tightly together. Each one produces a seed.

Dandelions flower in springtime.

The sepals cover the flower little by little.

The seeds form safely inside at the bottom of the flower.

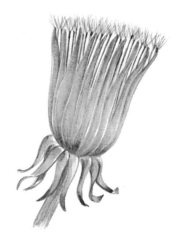

Each seed has its own stem topped by a feather called a pappus.

The pappi dry in the sun. Then they open into a pretty white pompom that you can blow away.

he pappi open. Each seed has its wn parachute.

The wind carries away the seeds.

he seeds land gently. They just ight...

grow into new dandelions. And it all starts over.

A FLOWER'S LIFE

Each different flower follows its own schedule. They unfold their petals, diffuse their scents and then close up at specific times.

Flowers unfold their petals to capture the sun's rays.

At night flowers breathe slowly with folded petals.

Blindweed flowers open at eight o'clock and close at two o'clock.

Water lilies open their petals at 7 a.m. and close at 4 p.m.

PLANTS STORE THEIR FOOD

Plants use their underground stores—roots, rhizomes, bulbs or tubers—to sprout and grow.

Tulip bulbs are large, onion-like buds that protect the stem.

Lily of the valley has a rhizome that produces new flowers every year.

Dahlia roots form flat clumps.

Dandelions' main roots are called taproots.

FLOWERS IN THE WOODS AND FIELDS

Listen carefully to these flowers' names. Can you guess which one blooms near the end of winter?

periwinkle

lily of the valley

heather

bluebell

violet

clover

daisy

anemone

primrose

snowdrop

buttercup

wild cherry

MEADOW FLOWERS

These flowers grow in meadows. The best-known one is the poppy which often grows in wheat fields.

cornflower

poppy

wild mustard

wild camomile

white-dead-nettle

medic

POND FLOWERS

Waterlilies sometime cover whole ponds. Irises, rushes and reeds grow close to the shore.

waterlily

iris

rushes

reeds

GARDEN FLOWERS

Thousands of different species of flowers grow on Earth.
We cultivate some of them to decorate our gardens.

1. roses
2. rhododendrons
3. anemones
4. dahlias
5. gladioluses
6. daffodils
7. lavender
8. carnations
9. petunias
10. clematis
11. tulips
12. geraniums
13. pansies
14. hydrangeas
15. lupins
16. daisies
17. lilies
18. delphiniums
19. lilies of the valley
20. narcissuses
21. asters

81

HEDGE FLOWERS

Fields and gardens are sometimes surrounded by thick hedges that protec
them from the wind. Flowers bloom in spring on some hedges.

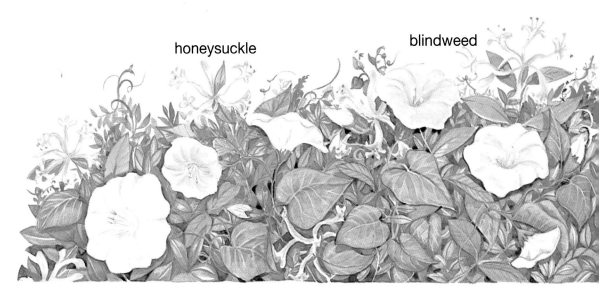

honeysuckle

blindweed

Blindweed flowers (shaped like trumpets) mingle with honeysuckle
blossoms (yellowish, with a strong scent).

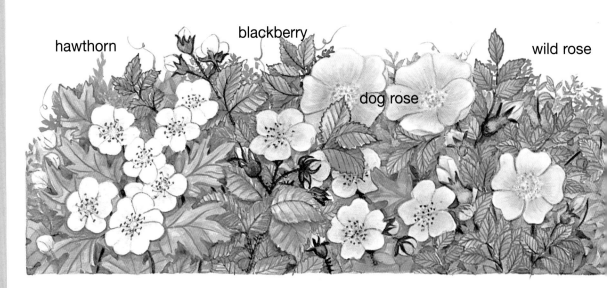

hawthorn

blackberry

wild rose

dog rose

You can see, from left to right, the flowers of hawthorn, blackberry
and wild rose bushes.

CACTI AND ROCK PLANTS

These plants have adapted to life in the deserts
and can live through long periods of drought.

These three prickly plants are cacti.
They store water that falls during the rainy season in their fat stems.

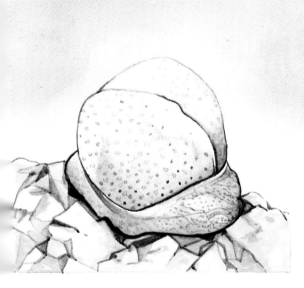

This rock plant is hard to spot
among the rocks.

Here is the rock plant's flower.
It looks like a blooming rock.

THE VENUS FLY-TRAP

Venus fly-traps are insectivorous plants. They live on soil that has little nutrition to offer so they prefer to catch insects.

The Venus fly-trap has spiny leaves...

that close around flies and trap them.

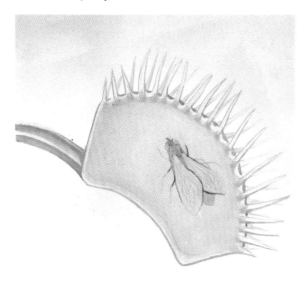

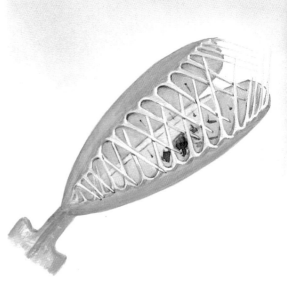

Then the Venus fly-trap slowly digests its prey.

Ten days later all that is left is the fly's skeleton.

PARASITE PLANTS

Parasite plants live off trees. Ivy deprives trees of air and suffocates them. Mistletoe steals their food.

Mistletoe uses a tiny sucker to drink the sap of trees.

Ivy uses sturdy tendrils to cling to tree bark.

Moss and lichen grow on the bark of certain trees.
Lichen grows best where the air is pure.

EDIBLE MUSHROOMS

The horn-of-plenty is a "good" mushroom—as you can guess from its name. You can eat all six mushrooms below.

horn-of-plenty

chanterelle

morel

cep

meadow mushroom

parasol mushroo

POISONOUS MUSHROOMS

These mushrooms contain deadly poison.
Never pick—or even touch—them.

boletus satanus

fly agaric

death cap

fool's mushroom

UNDERWATER PLANTS—SEAWEED

Rootless plants called seaweed live in the oceans.
They feed many different kinds of fish.

In the oceans seaweed comes in all kinds of shapes and colors.
Look closely at the seaweed below.
Can you find all three in the picture above?

bladderwrack   bladderwort   kelp

GOOD ADVICE

Here are a few tips on picking flowers. Careful!
Some flowers are protected by law—you aren't allowed to pick them.

Bring a box or basket to carry the flowers you pick.

Put your flowers in water right away.

Don't ever pull up the roots when you pick flowers.

Edelweiss flowers are very rare. You shouldn't pick them.

WHICH IS WHICH?
You've just read about a lot of plants. Do you remember these four?
Let's see...

Which of the four plants above is:
- a parasite that steals food from trees?
- a carnivorous plant that eats insects?
- a plant that you can eat?
- a dangerous plant that contains poison?

HOW TO MAKE A HERBARIUM FOR YOUR FLOWERS

Once your herbarium is ready, ask an adult to write the name of each flower and where it was picked next to it.

Chose one or two good examples of each flower.

Lay each flower between two sheets of newspaper.

Put a heavy pile of books on the newspaper for eight days.

Carefully glue the dry flowers onto the pages of a notebook.

NATURE BOY
Draw a large boy on a piece of thin cardboard.
Decorate him with flowers, grass and other things you have found outside.

dry grass for his hat

a stem for his necklace

dried flowers for his sweater

Spread glue on his pants and pour sand onto the glue.

a tube of glue

sand

WEATHER

FROM WATER TO CLOUDS

Look at the countryside below—the arrows show where the drops of water that make clouds come from.

High in the sky, water vapor meets cold air and forms tiny drops of water that group close together to make clouds.

The sun heats the water and turns it into vapor.

the sea

a pond

The leaves of trees, flowers and plants also produce water that turns into vapor and makes clouds.

river

PETER IS MAKING A CLOUD!

Peter and his father are experimenting.
You can do the same thing—if an adult helps you, of course.

First, they boil water in a pot.

Then dad pours the hot water into a glass bowl.

Then Peter fills a plate with ice cubes.

He puts the plate on top of the bowl.

When the water vapor meets the cold air under the plate it forms a could. You can see it best in the dark with a flashlight.

CHANGEABLE WATER!

Snow in winter, hail, rain and fog in spring—the drops of water change according to the temperature of the air.

RAIN

HAIL

Inside the clouds, the tiny drops of water stick together. They get so heavy that they fall to the ground as raindrops.

It is cold up there. The drops freeze inside the cloud, melt as they fall, and freeze once again to make hail.

SNOW

FOG

It is winter. The frozen drops cling to bits of dust as they fall. They form stars with six points that make snowflakes.

The warm and light air was full of water vapor. At night, the colder temperature makes it grow and fog forms.

WINTER FROST AND SUMMER DEW

Early mornings can be surprisingly beautiful with sparkling dew-covered plants or frosty white grass.

DEW

FROST

Tiny drops of water float in the air during the day. At night the air cools down and the water falls to the ground. This is early morning dew.

In winter, when it is cold enough, the dew freezes and turns into frost. The whole countryside is covered with white.

DIFFERENT KINDS OF CLOUDS

You've seen all different shapes of clouds in the sky. Did you know that each kind of cloud has its own name?

Cumulonimbus clouds carry rain.

Cirrostratus clouds announce bad weather.

Groups of tiny clouds are called altocumulus.

Cumulus clouds come with nice weather.

FROM BREEZE TO HURRICANE
The wind can blow gently or violently.
That's why it has so many different names.

BREEZES
Breezes are gentle winds that make grass and leaves flutter.
The sea is calm.

GALES
Gale winds blow hard. Look how they push the grass,
trees and boats and how they raise waves. What a storm!

HURRICANES

Hurricanes uproot trees and rip off roofs. They push huge waves—even tidal waves—to the shore!

TORNADOES

Watch out for tornadoes! They are violently spinning winds that move quickly and destroy everything in their paths.

BEFORE AND AFTER THE STORM

Look at the two pictures below. Can you list all the things that were changed by the storm?

THE STORM
It is very hot. Lightening strikes and you can hear thunder. Raindrops are about to fall from the dark clouds.

FLOOD!
So much rain fell during the storm that the fields are flooded. Look at the beautiful rainbow. How many colors does it have?

HOT AND COLD COUNTRIES

There are different climates on Earth. The sun shines very hotly over the deserts but it is always cold at the poles.

very hot regions

Camels can go without food or water for a long time in the desert.

North Pole

South Pole

Penguins live at the South Pole. At the poles, the winter night lasts six months!

THE FOUR SEASONS

What are these children doing? What are they wearing?
Can you guess which season it is in each picture?

WINTER

SPRING

SUMMER

AUTUMN

PREDICTING THE WEATHER

Meteorologists use several instruments to predict tomorrow's weather. Do you know what instruments they use?

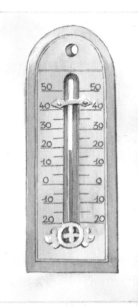

Weather vanes and windsocks show the direction of the wind.

Thermometers sho the temperature.

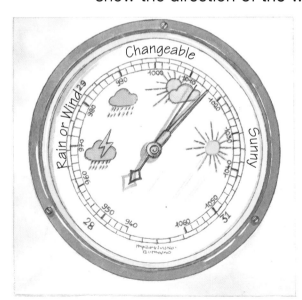

Barometers indicate what kind of weather it will be.

Satellites send us pictures of the clouds.

NATURE'S WEATHER BULLETIN

You can predict the weather too by
observing nature carefully.

When the sky is red at sunset
wind is on the way.

When the moon has a halo it
is going to rain.

When a storm is coming
swallows fly low in the sky.

When pine cones open up
sunshine is on the way.

MAKE A WEATHER CLOCK
Now it's your turn. You need colored cardboard, a metal fastener, address labels and glue.

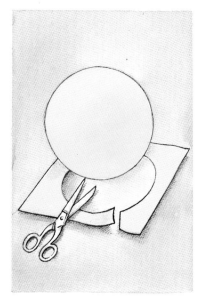

Cut out a large cardboard circle.

Copy these weather symbols onto the labels.

Stick them around the edges of your circle.

Cut an arrow out of thick cardboard.

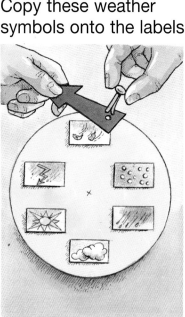

Attach the arrow to the center of the clock.

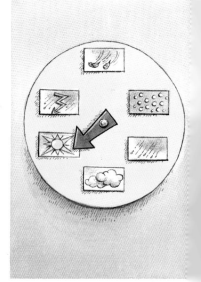

Every morning point the arrow of your weather map to the day's weather

WATER

WATER'S LONG VOYAGE

1. When the snow melts water flows down the mountains and off the glaciers.
2. The water in the streams flows down the mountains.
3. The stream becomes a small river.
4. Small rivers join larger rivers.
5. The river water mixes with sea water in estuaries.
6. Water evaporates and rises to form clouds.
7. The clouds meet cold air and rain or snow falls and the voyage starts all over.

Most water evaporates from the oceans but it also evaporates from rivers, fields, forests and factories.

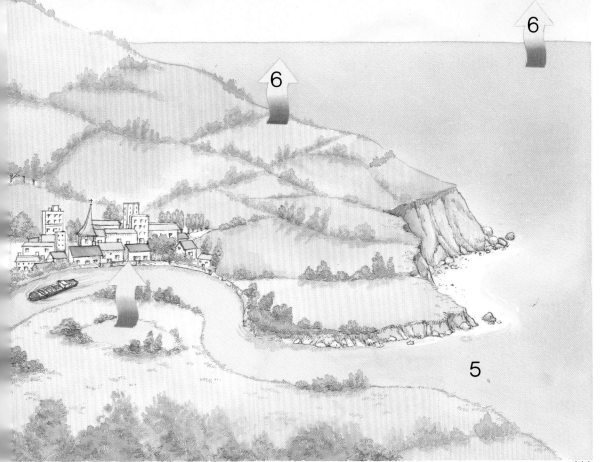

WATER IS POWERFUL

Have you ever seen waves knock down a sand castle?
Water is very strong. Look at just some of what it can do.

Waves crash so hard into cliffs that they can break off
huge rocks after several years.

Underground rivers dig caves and
surface in the form of springs.

Rivers can dig canyons
through mountains.

ICE FLOES—A HUGE STOCK OF WATER

The sea at the poles is frozen ice floes. If they melted the level of the oceans would rise and there would be lots of flooding!

This floating mountain of ice is an iceberg. Waves have carried it away from the ice floe. You can only see its tip—the rest is hidden under water.

These tiny icebergs make strange grumbling noises when they bump into each other.

TIDES

The sea recedes for six hours until it is low tide.
You can find shellfish, shrimp and seaweed.

Then the sea moves in for six hours until it is high tide.
Look at all the changes on the beach!

SOLID? LIQUID? STEAM?

Water is a liquid—you can pour it. When it is very cold it freezes and becomes solid. It turns into steam and disappears when heated.

t an ice tray full of water
the freezer.

The water is now solid.
What pretty ice cubes!

ur water onto a plate.
ter a few days...

the plate will be empty—the water
has evaporated!

WE ALL NEED WATER TO LIVE
Imagine all the things we couldn't do without water.
What about plants and animals?

Animals drink river water.

We drink water to quench our thirst.

We need water to wash ourselves.

Plants wither and die without water.

Water provides energy thanks to dams.

Water cools down the reactors in nuclear power plants.

Many animals and plants live underwater.

Water lets us transport people and goods easily.

ENDANGERED WATER

We all know how important water is but people still dump lots of things in it that make it dirty and undrinkable.

Factories sometimes spit out dangerous chemicals.

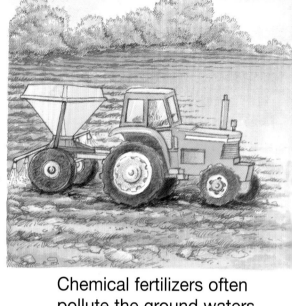

Chemical fertilizers often pollute the ground waters.

When oil spills in the ocean it causes an oil slick that kills birds and fish.

Some soaps contain toxic chemicals that end up in rivers and oceans.

ROCKS
AND LANDFORMS

AN ERUPTING VOLCANO

This mountain is spitting out rocks and ash—it is a volcano.
A river of burning lava is pouring down its slopes.

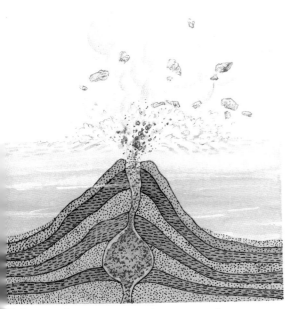

This underwater volcano gets bigger every time it erupts.

This volcano grew up above the surface. It will become an island.

The crater of this extinct volcano has filled with rainwater.

These volcanoes are covered with vegetation. Will they wake up?

YOUNG OR OLD MOUNTAINS?
Did you know that young mountains keep growing
and are pushed up from the center of the earth?

These mountains are forty million years old. Even so,
they are "young" mountains with pointy summits and steep slopes.

These mountains are much older. Snow, wind and rain
have rounded down their summits.

COASTLINES
Waves crash into the coasts at high tide and carve out
sandy beaches, cliffs and rocky coastlines.

Wind has formed sand dunes
that hold back the waves.

This beach is surrounded
by tall cliffs.

Waves have smoothed
the pebbles on this beach.

Here, the sea has cut out
rocks in all different sizes.

THE SEA BOTTOM

Here are two underwater landscapes. The top one is in shallow waters.
The bottom one is under much deeper waters.

Seaweed and fish live in the sand or on the rocks several feet under the surface.

It is very dark in the depths of the oceans. Strange fish live here. There are also deep holes called abysses.

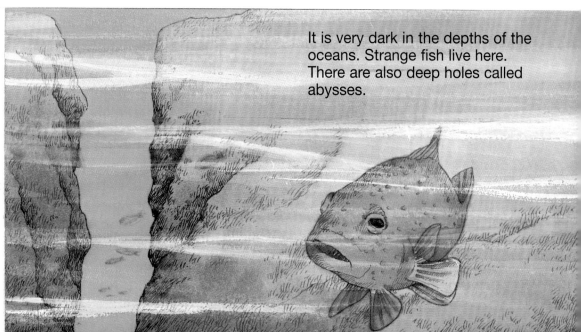

WATER AND WIND CARVE THE EARTH

Water digs the ground. Wind carries dust that wears away cliffs.
The landscape is constantly changing.

A long time ago a river dug this hole with high walls. It is called a canyon.

What a strange sight! Water wore down and carried away the soft rock and carved these beautiful "fairy chimneys" out of harder rock.

PLAIN OR PLATEAU?
Plains and plateaus are stretches of nearly flat land.
Men farm and raise animals on them.

Here is a plain. It is at low altitude.
Rivers have only dug into the land a little bit.

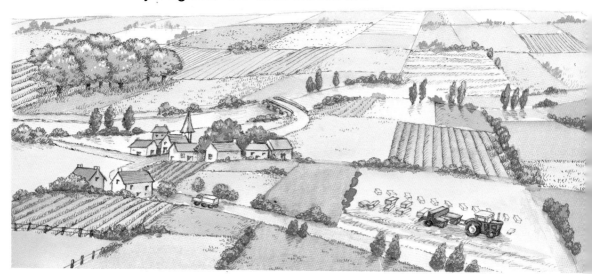

Plateaus are at medium or high altitudes.
They are cut by deep valleys.

SAND DUNES

Have you ever climbed a sand dune?
They can be very tall in the desert. They are sand mountains!

The wind carries sand in the desert.
It drops its sand when it bumps into an obstacle.

Little by little a new sand dune grows. It will get taller
and taller—if the wind doesn't carry it away.

ROCKS ARE USEFUL

Do you know the names of these rocks? Look closely.
You might have seen them before—or even used them.

Granite shines in the sun. It is sometimes used to build houses.

A blue-gray rock, **slate,** sometimes covers roofs.

Pumice stone can float and even clean things.

Marble comes in different color and is often carved and polishe

PRECIOUS GEMS

These rocks are dug out of the ground. Then they are cut and polished so that they shine. What pretty jewelry!

SAPPHIRE

EMERALD

RUBY

DIAMOND

TURQUOISE

AQUAMARINE

WHERE DOES COAL COME FROM?

People used to heat their houses by burning a black rock—coal—in stoves

Millions of years ago water covered the forests.

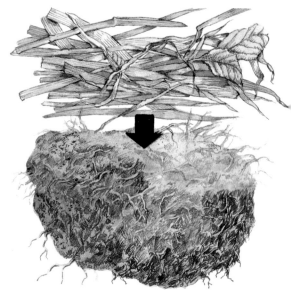

Branches and leaves rotted and became peat.

Crushed under rocks and dirt, the peat became coal.

Nowadays, people dig coal out of coal mines.

WHERE DOES OIL COME FROM?

Do you know what "black gold" is? It is oil. It is used to make gasoline.
It is millions of years old.

1

Small animals decomposed under water.

2

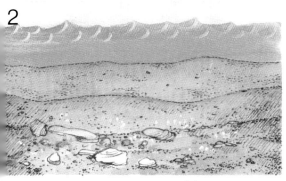

The sludge turned into petroleum and filled the rocks.

3

They mixed with the sand to form a kind of sludge.

an on-land oil well

If we poke a hole through the rock into a pocket of oil it spouts to the surface.

off-shore oil drilling

an off-shore oil well

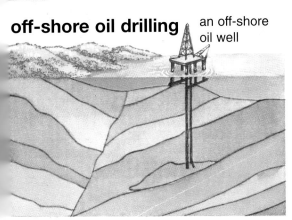

p. de titre tachée CG. 02-08